All Rights Reserved
All rights reserved. No part of this book may be reproduced in any form on or
by an electronic or mechanical
means, including information storage and retrieval systems, without
permission in writing from the publisher,
except by a reviewer who may quote brief passages in a review

Author
J B Moore

Ready,
Set,
Motivate,
Goal!

Ready, Set, Motivate, Goal!

Ready, Set, Motivate, Goal is a goal-setting journal designed to provide you with the steps to start goal setting. This journal is simple enough to allow anyone to set goals and achieve them. Why do I need to set goals? Setting goals does several things:

- Identifies your purpose in life.
- Triggers new behaviors.
- Guides your focus.
- Measures your progress.
- Gets you motived.
- Keeps you on track.

How do you start goal planning?

- Think of what you want to achieve in life.
- Think of the steps you need to take to achieve the things you want.
- Write down your goals.
- Create an action plan.
- Take action.
- Start succeeding toward your achievements.

What type of goal planning should I do?

- Daily
- Weekly
- Monthly
- Short-term goals planning
- Long-term goals planning

What type of goals do I need to set?

There's more than one answer to goal setting. However, SMART goals has been a proven go to method.

SMART Goals
S-Specific
M-Measurable
A-Achievable
R-Realistic
T-Within a Timeframe

Following this method allows you to create goals that are designed with your specific needs in mind. Keeping with the steps of this method you are setting goals that are realistic but also achievable.

Inside you will find the following:

- **Daily Goal Sheets.** Designed to help you set 3 daily goals. Also 1 daily reminder of gratitude.
- **Daily Accountability Sheets.** These sheets are designed to help you celebrate the achievement of your goals. It will also assist in learning what's working in your goal setting journey and what's not working. Learning what isn't working for you will allow you to reset and start over.
- **Monthly Planner Sheets.** You can set goals you want to achieve within the month or by the following month.
- **Yearly Planner Sheets.** These sheets will you to set long-term goals.
- **Reflections Sheets.** How do feel about the goals you've set? Is the process working for you? What are you learning about yourself? These sheets are designed to capture your thoughts and your reflections of this journey.

Best of luck on all your achievements!

Daily Goals Section One

Daily Goals

GRATITUDE REMINDER

GOAL-1

GOAL-2

GOAL-3

Daily Accountability

Goals Achieved

_____
_____
_____
_____
_____
_____

WHAT DID I OVERCOME?   ### WHAT DID I LEARN?

_____   _____
_____   _____
_____   _____
_____   _____

I AM THANKFUL FOR...

_____

Daily Goals

GRATITUDE REMINDER

GOAL-1

GOAL-2

GOAL-3

Daily Accountability

Goals Achieved

_____

_____

_____

_____

_____

WHAT DID I OVERCOME?   ### WHAT DID I LEARN?

_____	_____
_____	_____
_____	_____
_____	_____

I AM THANKFUL FOR...

_____

Daily Goals

GRATITUDE REMINDER

GOAL-1

GOAL-2

GOAL-3

Daily Accountability

Goals Achieved

_____
_____
_____
_____
_____
_____

WHAT DID I OVERCOME?

_____
_____
_____
_____

WHAT DID I LEARN?

_____
_____
_____
_____

I AM THANKFUL FOR...

_____

Daily Goals

GRATITUDE REMINDER

GOAL-1

GOAL-2

GOAL-3

Daily Accountability

Goals Achieved

_____

_____

_____

_____

_____

WHAT DID I OVERCOME?	WHAT DID I LEARN?
_____	_____
_____	_____
_____	_____
_____	_____

I AM THANKFUL FOR...

_____

Daily Goals

GRATITUDE REMINDER

GOAL-1

GOAL-2

GOAL-3

Daily Accountability

Goals Achieved

_____
_____
_____
_____
_____
_____

WHAT DID I OVERCOME?

_____
_____
_____
_____

WHAT DID I LEARN?

_____
_____
_____
_____

I AM THANKFUL FOR...

_____

Step by Step

Day by Day

Daily Goals

GRATITUDE REMINDER

GOAL-1

GOAL-2

GOAL-3

Daily Accountability

Goals Achieved

_____

_____

_____

_____

_____

WHAT DID I OVERCOME?   WHAT DID I LEARN?

_____   _____

_____   _____

_____   _____

_____   _____

I AM THANKFUL FOR...

_____

Daily Goals

GRATITUDE REMINDER

GOAL-1

GOAL-2

GOAL-3

Daily Accountability

Goals Achieved

_____
_____
_____
_____
_____
_____

WHAT DID I OVERCOME?   WHAT DID I LEARN?

_____   _____
_____   _____
_____   _____
_____   _____

I AM THANKFUL FOR. . .

_____

Daily Goals

GRATITUDE REMINDER

GOAL-1

GOAL-2

GOAL-3

Daily Accountability

Goals Achieved

_____

_____

_____

_____

_____

_____

WHAT DID I OVERCOME?   WHAT DID I LEARN?

_____   _____

_____   _____

_____   _____

_____   _____

I AM THANKFUL FOR. . .

_____

Daily Goals

GRATITUDE REMINDER

GOAL-1

GOAL-2

GOAL-3

Daily Accountability

Goals Achieved

_____
_____
_____
_____
_____
_____

WHAT DID I OVERCOME?   WHAT DID I LEARN?

_____   _____
_____   _____
_____   _____
_____   _____

I AM THANKFUL FOR...

_____

Daily Goals

GRATITUDE REMINDER

GOAL-1

GOAL-2

GOAL-3

Daily Accountability

Goals Achieved

_____
_____
_____
_____
_____

WHAT DID I OVERCOME?   WHAT DID I LEARN?

_____   _____
_____   _____
_____   _____
_____   _____

I AM THANKFUL FOR. . .

_____

Make Today Amazing

Daily Goals

GRATITUDE REMINDER

GOAL-1

GOAL-2

GOAL-3

Daily Accountability

Goals Achieved

_____
_____
_____
_____
_____
_____

WHAT DID I OVERCOME?

_____
_____
_____
_____

WHAT DID I LEARN?

_____
_____
_____
_____

I AM THANKFUL FOR. . .

_____

Daily Goals

GRATITUDE REMINDER

GOAL-1

GOAL-2

GOAL-3

Daily Accountability

Goals Achieved

_____

_____

_____

_____

_____

_____

WHAT DID I OVERCOME?   WHAT DID I LEARN?

_____   _____

_____   _____

_____   _____

_____   _____

I AM THANKFUL FOR. . .

_____

Daily Goals

GRATITUDE REMINDER

GOAL-1

GOAL-2

GOAL-3

Daily Accountability

Goals Achieved

_____
_____
_____
_____
_____
_____
_____

WHAT DID I OVERCOME?

_____
_____
_____
_____

WHAT DID I LEARN?

_____
_____
_____
_____

I AM THANKFUL FOR...

_____

Daily Goals

GRATITUDE REMINDER

GOAL-1

GOAL-2

GOAL-3

Daily Accountability

Goals Achieved

_____

_____

_____

_____

_____

_____

WHAT DID I OVERCOME?   ### WHAT DID I LEARN?

_____   _____

_____   _____

_____   _____

_____   _____

I AM THANKFUL FOR...

_____

Think It

Want It

Get It

Daily Goals

GRATITUDE REMINDER

GOAL-1

GOAL-2

GOAL-3

Daily Accountability

Goals Achieved

_____
_____
_____
_____
_____
_____

WHAT DID I OVERCOME?   WHAT DID I LEARN?

_____   _____
_____   _____
_____   _____
_____   _____

I AM THANKFUL FOR. . .

_____

Daily Goals

GRATITUDE REMINDER

GOAL-1

GOAL-2

GOAL-3

Daily Accountability

Goals Achieved

_____

_____

_____

_____

_____

_____

WHAT DID I OVERCOME?   ### WHAT DID I LEARN?

_____	_____
_____	_____
_____	_____
_____	_____

I AM THANKFUL FOR...

_____

Daily Goals

GRATITUDE REMINDER

GOAL-1

GOAL-2

GOAL-3

Daily Accountability

Goals Achieved

_____
_____
_____
_____
_____
_____

WHAT DID I OVERCOME?   WHAT DID I LEARN?

_____   _____
_____   _____
_____   _____
_____   _____

I AM THANKFUL FOR. . .

_____

Daily Goals

GRATITUDE REMINDER

GOAL-1

GOAL-2

GOAL-3

Daily Accountability

Goals Achieved

_____

_____

_____

_____

_____

_____

WHAT DID I OVERCOME?   WHAT DID I LEARN?

_____   _____

_____   _____

_____   _____

_____   _____

I AM THANKFUL FOR. . .

_____

Daily Goals

GRATITUDE REMINDER

GOAL-1

GOAL-2

GOAL-3

Daily Accountability

Goals Achieved

_____
_____
_____
_____
_____

WHAT DID I OVERCOME?   ### WHAT DID I LEARN?

_____   _____
_____   _____
_____   _____
_____   _____

I AM THANKFUL FOR...

_____

Daily Goals

GRATITUDE REMINDER

GOAL-1

GOAL-2

GOAL-3

Daily Accountability

Goals Achieved

_____
_____
_____
_____
_____

WHAT DID I OVERCOME?

_____
_____
_____
_____

WHAT DID I LEARN?

_____
_____
_____
_____

I AM THANKFUL FOR...

_____

Daily Goals

GRATITUDE REMINDER

GOAL-1

GOAL-2

GOAL-3

Daily Accountability

Goals Achieved

_____
_____
_____
_____
_____

WHAT DID I OVERCOME?   ### WHAT DID I LEARN?

_____   _____
_____   _____
_____   _____
_____   _____

I AM THANKFUL FOR. . .

_____

Daily Goals

GRATITUDE REMINDER

GOAL-1

GOAL-2

GOAL-3

Daily Accountability

Goals Achieved

_____
_____
_____
_____
_____
_____

WHAT DID I OVERCOME? ### WHAT DID I LEARN?

_____	_____
_____	_____
_____	_____
_____	_____

I AM THANKFUL FOR...

_____

Daily Goals

GRATITUDE REMINDER

GOAL-1

GOAL-2

GOAL-3

Daily Accountability

Goals Achieved

_____
_____
_____
_____
_____
_____

WHAT DID I OVERCOME?   WHAT DID I LEARN?

_____   _____
_____   _____
_____   _____
_____   _____

I AM THANKFUL FOR...

_____

Daily Goals

GRATITUDE REMINDER

GOAL-1

GOAL-2

GOAL-3

Daily Accountability

Goals Achieved

_____

_____

_____

_____

_____

WHAT DID I OVERCOME? **WHAT DID I LEARN?**

_____ _____

_____ _____

_____ _____

_____ _____

I AM THANKFUL FOR...

_____

Daily Goals

GRATITUDE REMINDER

GOAL-1

GOAL-2

GOAL-3

Daily Accountability

Goals Achieved

_____

_____

_____

_____

_____

_____

WHAT DID I OVERCOME?

_____

_____

_____

_____

WHAT DID I LEARN?

_____

_____

_____

_____

I AM THANKFUL FOR...

_____

Daily Goals

GRATITUDE REMINDER

GOAL-1

GOAL-2

GOAL-3

Daily Accountability

Goals Achieved

_____
_____
_____
_____
_____

WHAT DID I OVERCOME?   WHAT DID I LEARN?

_____   _____
_____   _____
_____   _____
_____   _____

I AM THANKFUL FOR...

_____

Daily Goals

GRATITUDE REMINDER

GOAL-1

GOAL-2

GOAL-3

Daily Accountability

Goals Achieved

_____
_____
_____
_____
_____
_____

WHAT DID I OVERCOME?   ### WHAT DID I LEARN?

_____   _____
_____   _____
_____   _____
_____   _____

I AM THANKFUL FOR...

_____

Daily Goals

GRATITUDE REMINDER

GOAL-1

GOAL-2

GOAL-3

Daily Accountability

Goals Achieved

_____
_____
_____
_____
_____
_____

WHAT DID I OVERCOME?   ### WHAT DID I LEARN?

_____   _____
_____   _____
_____   _____
_____   _____

I AM THANKFUL FOR...

_____

Daily Goals

GRATITUDE REMINDER

GOAL-1

GOAL-2

GOAL-3

Daily Accountability

Goals Achieved

_____
_____
_____
_____
_____
_____
_____

WHAT DID I OVERCOME?   WHAT DID I LEARN?

_____   _____
_____   _____
_____   _____
_____   _____

I AM THANKFUL FOR. . .

_____

Daily Goals

GRATITUDE REMINDER

GOAL-1

GOAL-2

GOAL-3

Daily Accountability

Goals Achieved

_____

_____

_____

_____

_____

WHAT DID I OVERCOME? WHAT DID I LEARN?

_____ _____

_____ _____

_____ _____

_____ _____

I AM THANKFUL FOR...

_____

Daily Goals

GRATITUDE REMINDER

GOAL-1

GOAL-2

GOAL-3

Daily Accountability

Goals Achieved

_____
_____
_____
_____
_____
_____

WHAT DID I OVERCOME?   WHAT DID I LEARN?

_____   _____
_____   _____
_____   _____
_____   _____

I AM THANKFUL FOR...

_____

Daily Goals Section Two

Daily Goals

GRATITUDE REMINDER

GOAL-1

GOAL-2

GOAL-3

Daily Accountability

Goals Achieved

_____
_____
_____
_____
_____
_____

WHAT DID I OVERCOME?

_____
_____
_____
_____

WHAT DID I LEARN?

_____
_____
_____
_____

I AM THANKFUL FOR...

_____

Daily Goals

GRATITUDE REMINDER

GOAL-1

GOAL-2

GOAL-3

Daily Accountability

Goals Achieved

_____
_____
_____
_____
_____

WHAT DID I OVERCOME?

_____
_____
_____
_____

WHAT DID I LEARN?

_____
_____
_____
_____

I AM THANKFUL FOR...

_____

Daily Goals

GRATITUDE REMINDER

GOAL-1

GOAL-2

GOAL-3

Daily Accountability

Goals Achieved

_____
_____
_____
_____
_____
_____

WHAT DID I OVERCOME?

_____
_____
_____
_____

WHAT DID I LEARN?

_____
_____
_____
_____

I AM THANKFUL FOR...

_____

You're Amazing

Daily Goals

GRATITUDE REMINDER

GOAL-1

GOAL-2

GOAL-3

Daily Accountability

Goals Achieved

_____
_____
_____
_____
_____
_____

WHAT DID I OVERCOME?

_____
_____
_____
_____

WHAT DID I LEARN?

_____
_____
_____
_____

I AM THANKFUL FOR...

_____

Daily Goals

GRATITUDE REMINDER

GOAL-1

GOAL-2

GOAL-3

Daily Accountability

Goals Achieved

_____

_____

_____

_____

_____

_____

WHAT DID I OVERCOME?	WHAT DID I LEARN?
_____	_____
_____	_____
_____	_____
_____	_____

I AM THANKFUL FOR. . .

_____

Daily Goals

GRATITUDE REMINDER

GOAL-1

GOAL-2

GOAL-3

Daily Accountability

Goals Achieved

_____
_____
_____
_____
_____
_____

WHAT DID I OVERCOME?

_____
_____
_____
_____

WHAT DID I LEARN?

_____
_____
_____
_____

I AM THANKFUL FOR...

_____

Daily Goals

GRATITUDE REMINDER

GOAL-1

GOAL-2

GOAL-3

Daily Accountability

Goals Achieved

_____
_____
_____
_____
_____
_____

WHAT DID I OVERCOME?

_____
_____
_____
_____

WHAT DID I LEARN?

_____
_____
_____
_____

I AM THANKFUL FOR. . .

_____

Daily Goals

GRATITUDE REMINDER

GOAL-1

GOAL-2

GOAL-3

Daily Accountability

Goals Achieved

___

___

___

___

___

WHAT DID I OVERCOME?

___

___

___

___

WHAT DID I LEARN?

___

___

___

___

I AM THANKFUL FOR...

___

Daily Goals

GRATITUDE REMINDER

GOAL-1

GOAL-2

GOAL-3

Daily Accountability

Goals Achieved

_____
_____
_____
_____
_____
_____

WHAT DID I OVERCOME?

_____
_____
_____
_____

WHAT DID I LEARN?

_____
_____
_____
_____

I AM THANKFUL FOR...

_____

Daily Goals

GRATITUDE REMINDER

GOAL-1

GOAL-2

GOAL-3

Daily Accountability

Goals Achieved

_____
_____
_____
_____
_____
_____

WHAT DID I OVERCOME?   WHAT DID I LEARN?

_____   _____
_____   _____
_____   _____
_____   _____

I AM THANKFUL FOR...

_____

Daily Goals

GRATITUDE REMINDER

GOAL-1

GOAL-2

GOAL-3

Daily Accountability

Goals Achieved

_____
_____
_____
_____
_____

WHAT DID I OVERCOME?   WHAT DID I LEARN?

_____   _____
_____   _____
_____   _____
_____   _____

I AM THANKFUL FOR...

_____

Daily Goals

GRATITUDE REMINDER

GOAL-1

GOAL-2

GOAL-3

Daily Accountability

Goals Achieved

_____
_____
_____
_____
_____
_____

WHAT DID I OVERCOME?   WHAT DID I LEARN?

_____   _____
_____   _____
_____   _____
_____   _____

I AM THANKFUL FOR...

_____

Daily Goals

GRATITUDE REMINDER

GOAL-1

GOAL-2

GOAL-3

Daily Accountability

Goals Achieved

_____
_____
_____
_____
_____
_____

WHAT DID I OVERCOME?   ### WHAT DID I LEARN?

_____	_____
_____	_____
_____	_____
_____	_____

I AM THANKFUL FOR...

_____

Daily Goals

GRATITUDE REMINDER

GOAL-1

GOAL-2

GOAL-3

Daily Accountability

Goals Achieved

_____
_____
_____
_____
_____

WHAT DID I OVERCOME?   WHAT DID I LEARN?

_____   _____
_____   _____
_____   _____
_____   _____

I AM THANKFUL FOR...

_____

Daily Goals

GRATITUDE REMINDER

GOAL-1

GOAL-2

GOAL-3

Daily Accountability

Goals Achieved

_____
_____
_____
_____
_____
_____

WHAT DID I OVERCOME?

_____
_____
_____
_____

WHAT DID I LEARN?

_____
_____
_____
_____

I AM THANKFUL FOR...

_____

Daily Goals

GRATITUDE REMINDER

GOAL-1

GOAL-2

GOAL-3

Daily Accountability

Goals Achieved

_____
_____
_____
_____
_____
_____

WHAT DID I OVERCOME?   WHAT DID I LEARN?

_____	_____
_____	_____
_____	_____
_____	_____

I AM THANKFUL FOR...

_____

Chase Your Stars

Daily Goals

GRATITUDE REMINDER

GOAL-1

GOAL-2

GOAL-3

Daily Accountability

Goals Achieved

_____

_____

_____

_____

_____

WHAT DID I OVERCOME?	WHAT DID I LEARN?
_____	_____
_____	_____
_____	_____
_____	_____

I AM THANKFUL FOR. . .

_____

Daily Goals

GRATITUDE REMINDER

GOAL-1

GOAL-2

GOAL-3

Daily Accountability

Goals Achieved

_____
_____
_____
_____
_____

WHAT DID I OVERCOME?

_____
_____
_____

WHAT DID I LEARN?

_____
_____
_____

I AM THANKFUL FOR...

_____

Daily Goals

GRATITUDE REMINDER

GOAL-1

GOAL-2

GOAL-3

Daily Accountability

Goals Achieved

_____
_____
_____
_____
_____
_____

WHAT DID I OVERCOME?

_____
_____
_____
_____

WHAT DID I LEARN?

_____
_____
_____
_____

I AM THANKFUL FOR...

_____

Daily Goals

GRATITUDE REMINDER

GOAL-1

GOAL-2

GOAL-3

Daily Accountability

Goals Achieved

_____
_____
_____
_____
_____

WHAT DID I OVERCOME?

_____
_____
_____
_____

WHAT DID I LEARN?

_____
_____
_____
_____

I AM THANKFUL FOR...

_____

Daily Goals

GRATITUDE REMINDER

GOAL-1

GOAL-2

GOAL-3

Daily Accountability

Goals Achieved

_____

_____

_____

_____

_____

WHAT DID I OVERCOME?	WHAT DID I LEARN?
_____	_____
_____	_____
_____	_____
_____	_____

I AM THANKFUL FOR. . .

_____

Daily Goals

GRATITUDE REMINDER

GOAL-1

GOAL-2

GOAL-3

Daily Accountability

Goals Achieved

_____
_____
_____
_____
_____
_____

WHAT DID I OVERCOME?

_____
_____
_____
_____

WHAT DID I LEARN?

_____
_____
_____
_____

I AM THANKFUL FOR...

_____

Daily Goals

GRATITUDE REMINDER

GOAL-1

GOAL-2

GOAL-3

Daily Accountability

Goals Achieved

_____

_____

_____

_____

_____

WHAT DID I OVERCOME?	WHAT DID I LEARN?
_____	_____
_____	_____
_____	_____
_____	_____

I AM THANKFUL FOR...

_____

Daily Goals

GRATITUDE REMINDER

GOAL-1

GOAL-2

GOAL-3

Daily Accountability

Goals Achieved

_____
_____
_____
_____
_____
_____

WHAT DID I OVERCOME?

_____
_____
_____
_____

WHAT DID I LEARN?

_____
_____
_____
_____

I AM THANKFUL FOR...

_____

Daily Goals

GRATITUDE REMINDER

GOAL-1

GOAL-2

GOAL-3

Daily Accountability

Goals Achieved

_____

_____

_____

_____

_____

WHAT DID I OVERCOME?   WHAT DID I LEARN?

_____   _____

_____   _____

_____   _____

_____   _____

I AM THANKFUL FOR. . .

_____

Daily Goals

GRATITUDE REMINDER

GOAL-1

GOAL-2

GOAL-3

Daily Accountability

Goals Achieved

_____
_____
_____
_____
_____
_____

WHAT DID I OVERCOME?	WHAT DID I LEARN?
_____	_____
_____	_____
_____	_____
_____	_____

I AM THANKFUL FOR...

_____

Daily Goals

GRATITUDE REMINDER

GOAL-1

GOAL-2

GOAL-3

Daily Accountability

Goals Achieved

_____
_____
_____
_____
_____
_____

WHAT DID I OVERCOME?

_____
_____
_____
_____

WHAT DID I LEARN?

_____
_____
_____
_____

I AM THANKFUL FOR...

_____

Reinvent Yourself

Daily Goals

GRATITUDE REMINDER

GOAL-1

GOAL-2

GOAL-3

Daily Accountability

Goals Achieved

_____
_____
_____
_____
_____
_____

WHAT DID I OVERCOME?   WHAT DID I LEARN?

_____   _____
_____   _____
_____   _____
_____   _____

I AM THANKFUL FOR. . .

_____

Daily Goals

GRATITUDE REMINDER

GOAL-1

GOAL-2

GOAL-3

Daily Accountability

Goals Achieved

_____

_____

_____

_____

_____

WHAT DID I OVERCOME?   WHAT DID I LEARN?

_____   _____

_____   _____

_____   _____

_____   _____

I AM THANKFUL FOR...

_____

Daily Goals

GRATITUDE REMINDER

GOAL-1

GOAL-2

GOAL-3

Daily Accountability

Goals Achieved

_____
_____
_____
_____
_____
_____

WHAT DID I OVERCOME?   WHAT DID I LEARN?

_____   _____
_____   _____
_____   _____
_____   _____

I AM THANKFUL FOR...

_____

Daily Goals

GRATITUDE REMINDER

GOAL-1

GOAL-2

GOAL-3

Daily Accountability

Goals Achieved

_____
_____
_____
_____
_____
_____

WHAT DID I OVERCOME?	WHAT DID I LEARN?
_____	_____
_____	_____
_____	_____
_____	_____

I AM THANKFUL FOR...

_____

Monthly Goal Section

Monthly Goal Planner

MONTH:

MON	TUES	WED	THU	FRI	SAT	SUN

MONTHLY GOALS

1.

2.

3.

NOTES

○ _____

○ _____

○ _____

○ _____

○ _____

Monthly Goal Planner

MONTH:

MON	TUES	WED	THU	FRI	SAT	SUN

MONTHLY GOALS

1.
2.
3.

NOTES

○ _____
○ _____
○ _____
○ _____
○ _____

Monthly Goal Planner

MONTH:

MON	TUES	WED	THU	FRI	SAT	SUN

MONTHLY GOALS

1.

2.

3.

NOTES

○ _____

○ _____

○ _____

○ _____

○ _____

Monthly Goal Planner

MONTH:

MON	TUES	WED	THU	FRI	SAT	SUN

MONTHLY GOALS

1.
2.
3.

NOTES

○ _____
○ _____
○ _____
○ _____
○ _____

Monthly Goal Planner

MONTH:

MON	TUES	WED	THU	FRI	SAT	SUN

MONTHLY GOALS

1.
2.
3.

NOTES

○ _____
○ _____
○ _____
○ _____
○ _____

Monthly Goal Planner

MONTH:

MON	TUES	WED	THU	FRI	SAT	SUN

MONTHLY GOALS

1.

2.

3.

NOTES

○ _____

○ _____

○ _____

○ _____

○ _____

Monthly Goal Planner

MONTH:

MON	TUES	WED	THU	FRI	SAT	SUN

MONTHLY GOALS

1.

2.

3.

NOTES

○ _____

○ _____

○ _____

○ _____

○ _____

Monthly Goal Planner

MONTH:

MON	TUES	WED	THU	FRI	SAT	SUN

MONTHLY GOALS

1.
2.
3.

NOTES

○ _____
○ _____
○ _____
○ _____
○ _____

Monthly Goal Planner

MONTH:

MON	TUES	WED	THU	FRI	SAT	SUN

MONTHLY GOALS

1.

2.

3.

NOTES

○ _____

○ _____

○ _____

○ _____

○ _____

Monthly Goal Planner

MONTH:

MON	TUES	WED	THU	FRI	SAT	SUN

MONTHLY GOALS

1.
2.
3.

NOTES

○ _____
○ _____
○ _____
○ _____
○ _____

Monthly Goal Planner

MONTH:

MON	TUES	WED	THU	FRI	SAT	SUN

MONTHLY GOALS

1.

2.

3.

NOTES

○ _____

○ _____

○ _____

○ _____

○ _____

Monthly Goal Planner

MONTH:

MON	TUES	WED	THU	FRI	SAT	SUN

MONTHLY GOALS

1.
2.
3.

NOTES

○ _____
○ _____
○ _____
○ _____
○ _____

Yearly Goal Section

LONG TERM GOALS

Year: _____

JANUARY	FEBRUARY	MARCH
APRIL	MAY	JUNE
JULY	AUGUST	SEPTEMBER
OCTOBER	NOVEMBER	DECEMBER

LONG TERM GOALS
Year: _____

JANUARY	FEBRUARY	MARCH

APRIL	MAY	JUNE

JULY	AUGUST	SEPTEMBER

OCTOBER	NOVEMBER	DECEMBER

LONG TERM GOALS

Year: _____

JANUARY	FEBRUARY	MARCH

APRIL	MAY	JUNE

JULY	AUGUST	SEPTEMBER

OCTOBER	NOVEMBER	DECEMBER

LONG TERM GOALS

Year:

JANUARY	FEBRUARY	MARCH

APRIL	MAY	JUNE

JULY	AUGUST	SEPTEMBER

OCTOBER	NOVEMBER	DECEMBER

LONG TERM GOALS

Year: _____

_____ JANUARY _____ _____ FEBRUARY _____ _____ MARCH _____

_____ APRIL _____ _____ MAY _____ _____ JUNE _____

_____ JULY _____ _____ AUGUST _____ _____ SEPTEMBER _____

_____ OCTOBER _____ _____ NOVEMBER _____ _____ DECEMBER _____

Personal Reflections Section

My Personal Reflections

My Personal Reflections

My Personal Reflections

My Personal Reflections

My Personal Reflections

My Personal Reflections

My Personal Reflections

My Personal Reflections

My Personal Reflections

www.ingramcontent.com/pod-product-compliance
Lightning Source LLC
Chambersburg PA
CBHW081615100526
44590CB00021B/3451